MW01089002

LIFE IN ANTARCTICA

Geography Lessons for 3rd Grade

Children's Explore the World Books

BABY PROFESSOR

EDUCATION KIDS

Speedy Publishing LLC

40 E. Main St. #1156

Newark, DE 19711

www.speedypublishing.com

Copyright 2017

All Rights reserved. No part of this book may be reproduced or used in any way or form or by any means whether electronic or mechanical, this means that you cannot record or photocopy any material ideas or tips that are provided in this book.

Antarctica is the continent around the South Pole. Who and what lives there, and what is their life like? Read on and find out!

South Sandwich
Islands (U.K.)

South Georgia
(U.K.)

South Orkney
Islands · ■ Orcadas (ARGENTINA)

Neumayer
(GERMANY)

SANAE IV
(SOUTH AFRICA)

Maitri
(INDIA)

Novo-
lazarevskaya
(RUSSIA)

Queen Maud Land

Syowa (JAPAN)

(RUSSIA)

Enderby
Land

Esperanza
(ARGENTINA)
Bernardo O'Higgins (CHILE)
Arturo Prat (CHILE)

Halley (U.K.)

Palmer (U.S.)
Vernadsky (UKRAINE)

Larsen Ice Shelf

Belgrano II (ARGENTINA)

Mawson (AUSTRALIA)

Rothera (U.K.)

San Martín
(ARGENTINA)

Berkner Island

Mac. Robertson
Land

Amery Ice Shelf

Alexander Island

Ronne
Ice Shelf

Palmer
Land

Zhong Shan (CHINA)
Progress (RUSSIA)
Davis (AUSTR.)

Peter Island

Ellsworth
Land

ANTARCTICA

South Pole Amundsen-Scott (U.S.)

Mirnyy (RUSSIA)

Shackleton
Ice Shelf

Vostok (RUSSIA)

Marie Byrd
Land

Ross
Ice Shelf

Concordia
(FRANCE and ITALY)

Wilkes Land

Casey
(AUSTR.)

McMurdo (U.S.)

Scott (N.Z.)

Victoria
Land

Dumont d'Urville
(FRANCE)

South Magnetic
Pole

Scott Island ·

Balleny
Islands

THE COLD CONTINENT

Antarctica is twice the size of Australia, but has such a hostile climate that it has very little animal or even plant life. Most of the land is covered by ice as much as several miles thick. It is the coldest and windiest environment on Earth, with the least annual precipitation of any continent.

PLANT LIFE

Millions of years ago, when the Earth was much warmer, Antarctica had thick vegetation. Now, since almost all the land is covered with ice and snow all year around, only about 1 percent of the continent is available for even the hardiest plants.

ANTARCTICA LEMAIRE CHANNEL

ANTARCTIC HAIR GRASS

However, where local conditions let the ground be ice-free for at least part of the year, there are some plants. Life is stubborn, and will take root wherever it can!

There are no bushes or trees, and only two types of flowering plant. These are Antarctic pearlwort and Antarctic hair grass.

If you look very closely at exposed rocks, though, you will see an interesting population of fungi, moss, and lichen, species that have adapted to survive the extreme cold. These plant species can live in tiny cracks and openings in sandstone and granite rocks.

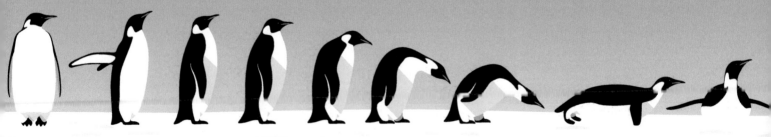

ANTARCTIC MOSS

ANTARCTIC FUR SEAL

ANIMAL LIFE

Most of the animals of Antarctica spend the coldest parts of the year elsewhere, migrating to South America, Africa, or Australia. Almost no species live on the continent year-round.

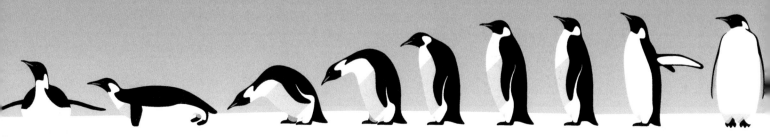

Those who spend the most time in Antarctica are aquatic mammals like penguins, seals, and whales. The penguins, in particular, come to traditional areas to have their chicks, and then return to the sea once the babies are old enough to swim and feed themselves.

PENGUINS ON THE SNOW

ANTARCTIC KRILL

Whales and other sea creatures depend for a large part of their diet on krill, tiny lobster-like creatures. Krill are the foundation of the Antarctic food chain.

Birds such as gulls, albatrosses, and skuas also visit and breed in Antarctica, though they avoid the continent during winter, when the weather is harshest.

GREAT SKUA

HUMAN LIFE

Unlike all the other continents, Antarctica has no indigenous people. Although Antarctica was once connected to all the other continents, it separated from them long before humans evolved. There has been no land connection from other parts of the world with Antarctica for about 35 million years.

Humans evolved about five million years ago in eastern Africa, and then spread to the rest of the world; but there was no easy way to get to Antarctica by then.

HUMAN EVOLUTION

ROUGH OCEAN

The climate is hostile and the oceans are rough and stormy, so even if someone had known Antarctica was out there across the water, it would have been almost impossible to reach the continent until modern times.

It was only around 1820 that sailing ships and navigation improved so people could sail south far enough to even see Antarctica from a distance. In the decades after that some people claimed to have visited the continent, but historians and scientists doubt their stories.

OLD SAILING SHIP

A TOURIST TAKING A PICTURE OF PENGUINS

Humans probably first reached Antarctica around 1899. And, of course, when they got there, they found there were no local people waiting to greet them or sell them souvenirs!

Most people who travel to Antarctica are either scientists or tourists.

In fact, travel to the continent is tightly controlled, both to protect its delicate environment and to protect people who might get into trouble or even die if they get to the continent without the right equipment or not in good enough shape to spend a long time far away from the nearest doctor.

If you tried to go to Antarctica on your own, and not as part of a scientific project or an approved tourist group, you would be breaking international laws and also the law of your own country.

SCIENTIST INSTALLING A WEATHER INSTRUMENT

RESEARCH STATION

SCIENTISTS

Scientists and researchers come to Antarctica for a season, or for up to two years, and live and work in research stations scattered around the continent. There are almost 70 such stations, and about half of them have year-round populations.

However, each station is very small. If you went there, you would have to be ready to spend six months or a year with fifty or fewer people as your whole community. It is sort of like going to spend time on the International Space Station: everything you are going to use, eat, and rely on has to come from outside, at great cost.

In all, Antarctica has about four thousand people in its science bases during the summer months, and as few as one thousand during the winter.

HOUSES IN ANTARCTICA

However, sometimes the ships that are due to come at the end of the summer to take people away can't make it because of bad weather and ice forming early, so people sometimes find they have to spend the winter in Antarctica when they didn't want to.

Some people in past years had bad luck with the weather, and had to spend as much as three continuous years in Antarctica.

They found it hard to survive the isolation and limited range of things they could do, and then found it hard to get used to civilization once they returned to it!

On average, the United States has the most people on Antarctica every year, averaging about 250 during the winter and over 1,500 in the summer. Australia, Russia, Argentina, and Chile all have hundreds of their scientists in Antarctica every year, and other countries have smaller numbers.

1951 - 2001

CHILEAN ANTARCTIC RESEARCH STATION

MCMURDO STATION, ANTARCTICA

ANTARCTIC SETTLEMENTS AND "NATIVES"

In the whole continent, the place that is the most like a town is the United States base at McMurdo Sound. And even here, the peak population in summer is about one thousand scientists and staff. It is really more like a military base than a town.

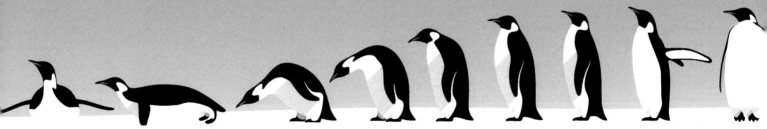

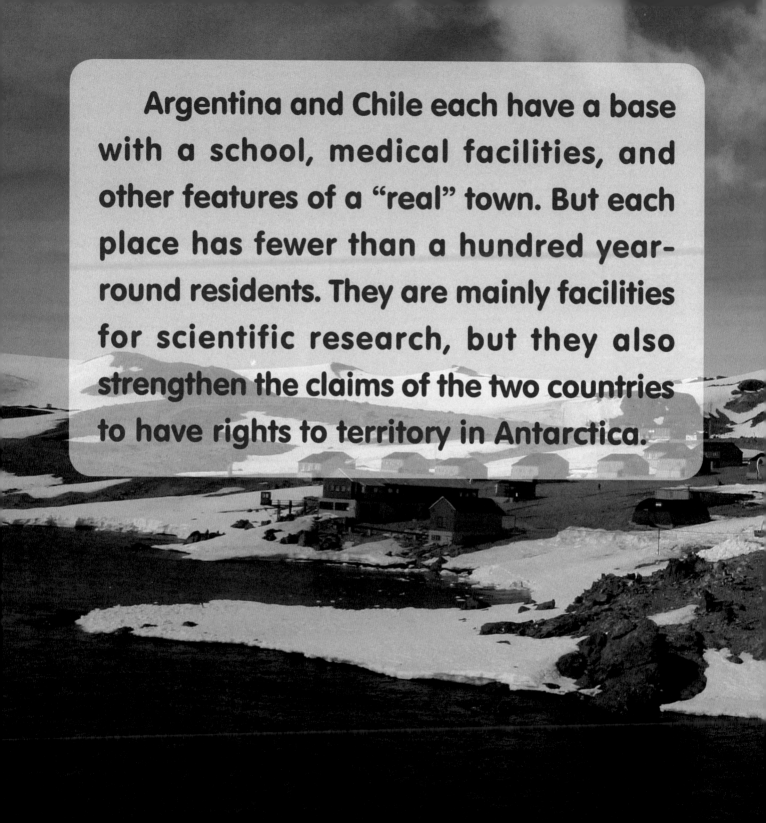

Argentina and Chile each have a base with a school, medical facilities, and other features of a "real" town. But each place has fewer than a hundred year-round residents. They are mainly facilities for scientific research, but they also strengthen the claims of the two countries to have rights to territory in Antarctica.

This is in preparation against a future time when the political agreement between nations to govern and protect the continent might change.

ARGENTINE RESEARCH STATION

In fact, in the 1970s both countries supported pregnant women who were willing to travel to Antarctica and have their babies there, so they could say those children were "natives" of Antarctica.

As many as ten children have been born in Antarctica. Emilio Marcos Palma, the first, is an Argentinian born there in 1978. In 1984, Juan Pablo Camacho was the first Chilean born on the continent. None of the "native Antarcticans" lives on the continent, though.

PREGNANT WOMAN IN SNOW

TOURISTS

During 2015-16, over 38,000 people visited Antarctica as tourists, down from the record of 47,000 in 2007-8. Large cruise ships are no longer allowed to travel to the continent because of the danger of oil spills, running onto uncharted rocks, or getting into a dangerous situation that would require an expensive rescue operation.

A MAN RIDING SNOWMOBILE

In the past one could only go to Antarctica by ship, over rough seas. It is now possible to fly from Chile to the Chilean base Villa las Estrellas, and then join a small vessel there to tour the Antarctic coast. Tourists can also take guided snowmobile and ski trips out from the base, and visit penguin rookeries and seabird colonies.

It is quite expensive to be an Antarctic tourist, and the scale of operations is small. For example, the "hotel" at Villa las Estrellas only has twenty rooms.

VILLA LAS ESTRELLAS

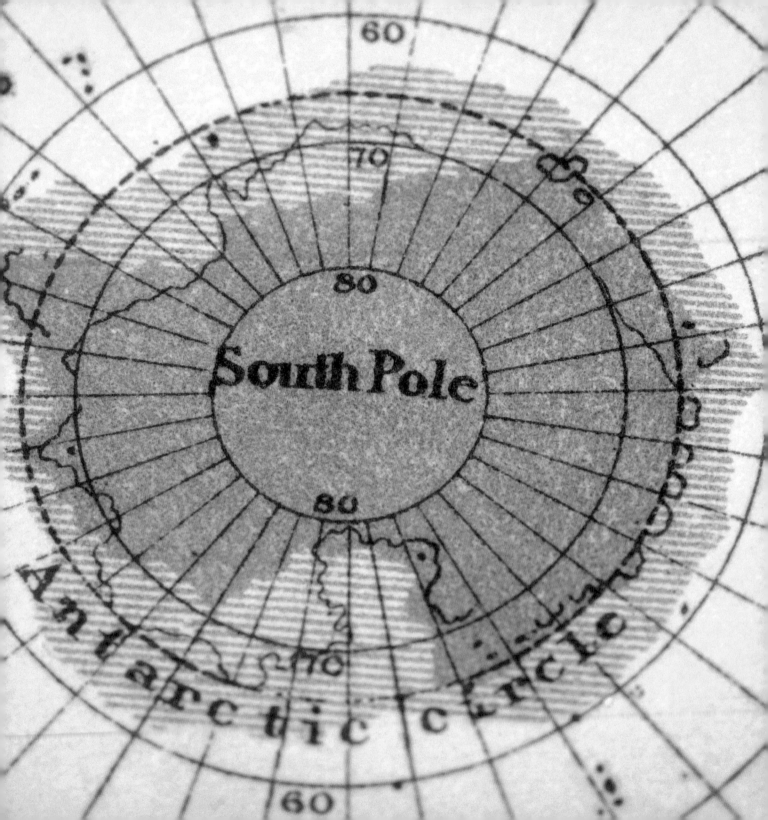

RACE TO THE SOUTH POLE

Explorers competed with each other to learn about Antarctica, even though nobody thought there would be anything like hidden cities of gold or dinosaurs, or other wonders you might find in fantasy stories. In particular, explorers were anxious to be the first to reach the South Pole.

The South Pole is not a physical thing. It is the southern point of the imaginary line through the center of the Earth around which the Earth rotates. The other end, of course, is the North Pole. You can learn about the North Pole in the Baby Professor book Can I See Santa at the North Pole?

Norwegian explorer Roald Amundsen was preparing to try to get to the North Pole in 1909, when he learned that American explorers Robert Peary and Frederick Cook both claimed to have reached that Pole.

ROALD AMUNDSEN

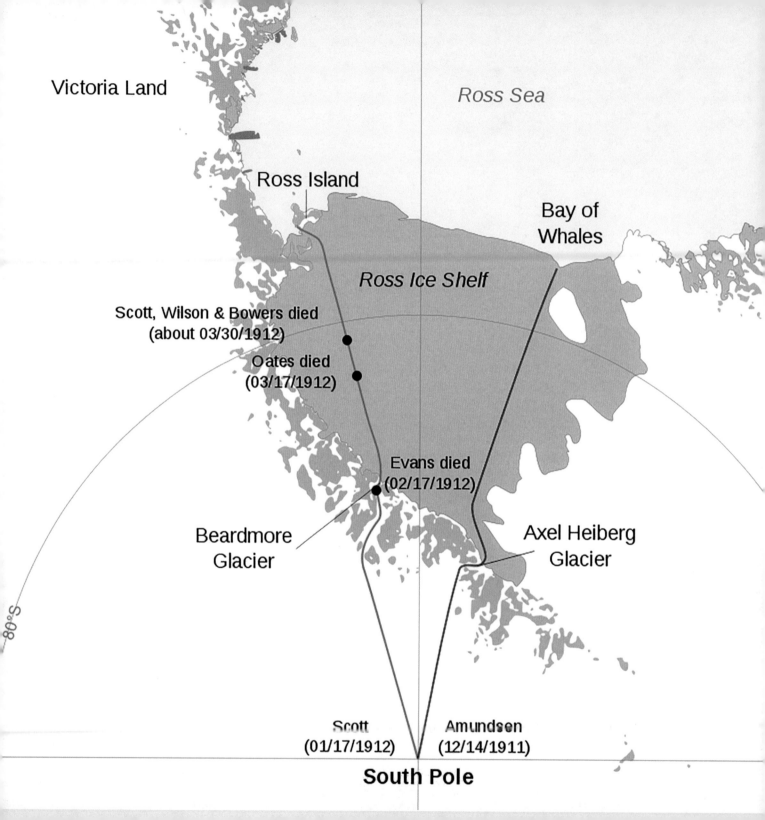

Amundsen then decided to change his plans and to tackle the South Pole.

He kept his plans a secret for a long time, afraid that his backers would not support him if they knew how his adventure had changed. He even let his crew think they were heading for the Arctic when they sailed in 1910, and only told them of the change of plans once the ship was at sea.

Amundsen and his team made good use of skis and sled-dogs, and were fortunate to find a glacier (now called the Axel Helberg Glacier) they could use to get up from the coastal lowlands into the interior plain of Antarctica. They arrived at the South Pole on December 14, 1911, beating a British group led by Robert Falcon Scott by about five weeks.

GROUP OF HUSKY SLED DOGS

THERE IS LIFE EVERYWHERE!

There is much more to learn about life on Earth in Baby Professor books like Who Lives in the Barren Desert? and Who Lives in a Tropical Rainforest?

You can find more interesting topics by reading other Baby Professor books and by searching the website of your favorite book retailer.

Visit

BABY PROFESSOR
EDUCATION KIDS

www.BabyProfessorBooks.com

to download Free Baby Professor eBooks
and view our catalog of new and exciting
Children's Books

Made in the USA
Middletown, DE
22 February 2020

85180944R00038